Softlie

...love poems spun into a storyline

KAYODE TAIWO OLLA

SYNCTERFACE™
Syncterface Media
London
www.syncterfacemedia.com

Softlie: love poems spun into a storyline
ISBN: 978-0-9569741-9-8
Copyright © December 2013 Kayode Taiwo Olla
All Rights Reserved

Published in the United Kingdom by

SYNCTERFACE™

Syncterface Media
London
www.syncterfacemedia.com
info@syncterfacemedia.com

Author Photograph: Deji Adepetu
Cover Photography: Abdullah Kolawole
Illustrations: David Ikhide

This book is printed on acid-free paper

Endorsements

Softlie... poetry with rhythmic finesse. Captivating love creed.

Ifeoluwapo Adeniyi,
Presenter and Socio-political Analyst,
SPLASH 105.5 FM, Ibadan, Nigeria

Love stands as a chimera; a mistaken sensory perception, but not anymore. Kayode Olla has given life to love and love to life with words that make the heart grope to reach the glimmering allure of the best gift available to humans.

Hannah Ojo,
Journalist at *The Nation* Newspaper, Lagos, Nigeria

Every one of us wishes to read a book that allows us to find ourselves. This is such a collection—filled with our voices conversing with our lovers, filled with the sort of experiences we have on our way to love. Olla is certainly a voice we have to listen to, henceforth.

Emmanuel Iduma,
Author of *Farad*

To the God of love, and

For Omotola

■

I have spun a song soft as a murmur of doves at noon…
I have offered you wild flowers with scents as strange as a sorcerer's eyes
I have offered you my wild flowers. Will you let them wither,
Finding distraction in the mayflies dancing?

Leopold Sedar Senghor, "I have spun a song…"

Foreword

SOFTLIE IS A FASCINATING COLLECTION OF LOVE POEMS, TEASED out in the form of narrative. The poet Kayode Olla is, without doubt, one of the greatly promising talents among young Nigerian writers of this century, having published his first full-length novel while studying English at Obafemi Awolowo University, Ile-Ife.

Ordinarily, the union of the sexes, whether in affection or hostility, is a vast pool which creative artists — poets, dramatists, musicians, painters and sculptors — from ancient times to the present, have drawn inspirations for their thematic concerns and style. Thus, a new work in this direction stands the risk of treading the familiar path without making much impression. What subtly but eloquently stands out in Kayode Taiwo Olla's *Softlie*, is its uncommon blend of the poetic with the narrative, and the melodic with the dramatic.

From poem to poem, the poet sustains a dialogic exchange between a lover and his partner, both ever longing for the consummation of their feelings in an oasis of affection. The reader's attention is firmly held and sustained from the beginning to the end of the collection through irony, pun, suspense and ellipsis.

The images in *Softlie* evoke cross-cultural experience of people in past and contemporary Africa. This enables the poet to consciously interject what seems to be private with the public and political. Hence, the collection travels on two roads of signification simultaneously and arrives at both destinations. The title of the collection—'Softlie,' testifies to this as it can be pronounced and invested with the meaning of 'softly' and it can also be rendered as 'soft lie,' knowing full well and being conscious of the fact that lies, intrigues and duplicity often constitute the Achilles' heel of love and politics. *Softlie* is therefore a richly endowed collection of poems that I find enticing with every reading and it is self-recommending.

Prof. Gbemisola Adeoti
Director,
Institute of Cultural Studies,
Obafemi Awolowo University,
Ile-Ife, Nigeria.

Preface

IT IS A USUAL THING FOR LOVE POEM COLLECTIONS TO HAVE their content poems as separate and distinct monologues, mostly with the same character (*the poet-persona*) in one collection 'voicing' each romantic address, each poem, all through the collection. It, however, occurs to me that if romances are narrated in fictions or acted in comedies—why not in poetry as well? I mean, why can't poetry, too, *tell a love story?!*

This collection of love poems is written in such a way that it forms a dramatic love story when you bridge the seeming gap between the poems. Each poem bears—or perhaps rather, is borne, by a particular character's voice. Each of the monologues is in form of an address, or a response to an address, or is simply a meditation; thus, giving the poems the dramatic semblance of dialogue and thought, and at the same time evoking to the reader a background of sequence of events.

SOFTLIE is intended to pleasantly delight as well as inspire, to softly evoke sweet emotions and as well provoke deep reflections—all in all merging into one blend the useful and the sweet; the didactic and the aesthetic.

So now, since each poem links to the next in a chain of plot, I suggest to the reader that at least a section should be completed in one sitting; it is a precaution for the reader not to lose track of the whole plot's flow. And so, I wish you a happy reading and pray that you have a truly fulfilled love life!

K. T. O.

Contents

iii.   Retrospection

iv.   Inflection

v.   Reflection

vi.   Perfection

vii.   Repression

Prelude

For you

To her who is mine

You are my precious jewel
I gave up many gems
for you!
You are my sweet angel
I waited these long days
for you!
You're my lovely lily
You're my priceless princess
You're my dew at dawn, my baby!
And I have written this piece
for you!

If ever you doubt whether you mean so much to me
remember please that many I bypassed —
for you!
If ever time tests your love so badly
remember please I spent the long days just

                              waiting for you!
For, you're my scented fountain
You're my sweet feelings
You're the sunshine on my flower, my baby!
And I have kept this song
for you!

I'll look in your eyes
and see me
You'll look in my eyes
and see you
I'll be the man you've dreamed of
You'll be the woman I've hoped for—
We will be our dreams come true,
you and me!
I'll be your heart; you'll be my throb
You'll be my heart; I'll be your throb—
We'll be two hearts merge into one,
yours and mine!
And this I have been praying these years
…For us!

i.   Inception

What lady is that, which doth enrich the hand of yonder knight?
O, she doth teach the torches to burn bright!
It seems she hungs upon the cheek of night
Like a rich jewel in an Ethiope's ear;
Beauty too rich for use, for earth too dear…
Did my heart love till now? forswear it, sight!
For I ne'er saw true beauty till this night.

Shakespeare, *Romeo and Juliet*

Funso gradually dropped his gaze to Yemisi's slender fingers on the
desk and took note that no wedding ring adorned her ring finger.
… [He] slowly raised his gaze a little bit; and Yemisi too. Her eyes met his.
Funso gave a slight smile. She chuckled and looked down immediately.

Kayode Taiwo Olla, *Sprouting Again**

---
* Olla, Kayode T. Sprouting Again. London: Syncterface Media, 2011. Print.

[ARẸMU]

Back to campus

Here, we see ourselves every week—
    maybe everyday.
We see ourselves around every day,
    so much we don't even 'see' ourselves!
We've met nowhere—
    pardon me, we meet everywhere.
We meet everywhere for work,
    so much we can only remember we've met
              somewhere before!
Everybody sees anybody—
    no, *manybodies*.
Everybody sees 'manybodies' here,
    so somebody can't just remember everybody
              when back home.
Universality they call this place—
    sorry, University!

I'm sorry, the break was short—
        erm, I mean, long.
The break was pretty long,
        and so I lost memory of faces.
No, the weeks before the break was tedious—
        you know, monotonous as usual.
The weeks before the break was monotonous—
        too bad I saw everybody and so couldn't
                        notice somebody!
Such is the universality—
        sorry, the university of life!

I didn't know I ever saw you
        till I didn't see you back a' home and
                        missed you!
I didn't know there is 'you' at all,
        thank goodness I replayed my
                        subconscious memory tape!
Here, we all can't notice the splendour of
                        our twinkles
        till we go out of this Universality and
                        realize what big stars we are!
So, welcome back.
        Erm, pleased to see your face—
        again!

[ARẸMU]

Let's walk

In the ballroom
partnering you—
I the he, you the she...
In the ballroom
dancing the tango—
I with you, you with me...
In the ballroom
taking calculated steps
spinning systematically
you placing your hand in mine ceremonially...
In the ballroom dancing
not even our proximity is potent enough
to make us become close.

Ah, please come with me
away from the formality and the artificiality
of ballrooms dancing
this acquaintanceship
this formal friendship—
yes, to the intimacy and close relationship
in free walking
in love beyond law!

Come with me to nature!
Come with me to song!
We will have the village green
for 'ballroom'
We will have the birdsong
for music
We will have the turtledove pairs
for fellow dancers — no, walkers.

> Come with me to nature
> Come with me to song
> We will have the turtledove pairs
> for fellow dancers
> We will have the turtledove pairs
> for fellow walkers

…and now please, Arẹwa[*]
put your hand in mine
look into my eyes…

let's walk.

---

[*] Beautiful lady.

[ARẸWA]

Pure love

Lilies of the savannah scarcely fade
In their pure whites
The river bird's call
Is clear all day
The river bird's call
Is pure all night
Lilies of the savannah scarcely fade
In their pure whites:
I wish we still have pure love nowadays!

Ripples in clear still waters
Simply say they have nothing to hide
The Ifẹ smith's bronze
Only glows the purest gloss
The Benin smith's brass
Only gleams the purest sheens
Ripples in clear still waters
Simply say they have nothing to hide:

Ah I wish we have pure motives and pure minds
Pure hearts and pure love
        And chaste kisses,
                And friendly pecks,
                        And saintly lips…
And purely platonic relationships!

[ARẸMU]

If it is love...

If it is the flare of infatuation
guy will see gal as a must-get date
If it is the fire of lust
dude will see babe as a sexual means
If it is the flicker of liking
boy will see girl as an acquaintance
But if it is the flame of love
I will see you as my heart!

If it is love, love genuine, unfeigned
it can't be faked, won't be stained
If it is love, love strong and fervent
many waters can't it quench
If it is love, love pure, real and true
it does fill the whole of you —
If it is love, hmm, if it is love
Then I'll say it's from above!

> If it is the flare of infatuation
> guy will see gal as a must-get date
> If it is the fire of lust
> dude will see babe as a sexual means
> If it is the flicker of liking
> boy will see girl as an acquaintance…

but Love It is...
And I see you as my heart!

[ARĘWA]

We all want it

The hardest, stoniest heart
Has a soft spot
The most stoic body
Inwardly yearns for a loving caress
Men's deepest wish
Men's deepest longing
Men's deepest desire
Is not power or prestige —
I've seen it is to feel loved!
　　　We all want it so badly!

Yes, behind our own stony faces
We've got pretty smiling dimples
Wishing to be unmasked
Behind our firmly shut lips
We've got some real chuckle
Longing to be unlocked
Our sincerest urge
Our sincerest appetite
Our sincerest desire
Is not to have sexual enjoyment—
Rather, to have the happiness of being truly loved!
      We all want it so badly!

So if we so badly want to be loved
Why not love ourselves the right way?—
And deeply too!
And our biggest gift
Our biggest gem
Our biggest gesture
      Can only be love,
      I guess!

[ARẸMU]

Awẹlẹwa

Ah what a smile sweet
What a smile serene
What a smile of great sweetness…

Down the path she walked to the river
an earthen pot on her bare shoulder
and around her body she had a wrapper

Captivated by her natural beauty, I beamed
and in her eyes, too, was a loving gleam
and in her eyes, too, was a loving gleam

Her plain *ankara* caught my eyes!
Ah what charming beauty —
yet rustic!
What charming beauty —
yet scarcely embellished by cosmetics!
And yet looked a goddess
of unaltered natural beauty!

what a smile sweet
what a smile serene
what a smile of great sweetness
That has won my heart!

And her African hair,
her shiny black hair she wore in plaits
and I wished to call her and chat
And so I said, You're beautiful dear!
Yes, she is beautiful; and I call her Dear!

        …Oh no —
but just a curt and cute 'thank you sir'
was her only answer!
And on she went
and off she went
leaving me there!
Oh no…
just a curt and cute 'thank you sir'
was her only answer!
And on she went
and off she went…
        leaving me there!

...And there alone I stood with gaping mouth
Wondering at the scarce meld of
                              Nature an' Nurture!
Pondering the rare blend of
                              Culture an' Nature!
And the sheer fuse of
                              Beauty... and Character!

        and for three markets*
        i was hard trying
        to win the heart
        of my maiden:
        just to discover,
        after winning,
        that she had been falling for me
        since seven!

---

* Market weeks. A market week of any particular marketplace or region in traditional Yoruba
communities, is a difference between two market days which may vary from like 4 days to up
to, say, 8 or even 16 days.

ii. Expressions

Time was away and somewhere else,
There were two glasses and two chairs
And two people with one pulse.

Louis MacNeice, *Holes in the Sky,* **"Meeting Point"**

[THE AYEK'OOTỌ BIRD*]

Beauty is...

Beauty is the lustre reflected
by a beholder's eye on his mind
It is the charm that enchants
the wandering eyes and the still mind
It is powerful magnetism that attracts
the opposite poles of the Creator's Man
It is a maiden's spell so potent
that it can capture a manly man's heart...
And beauty is only skin-deep
        but real and surpassing beauty
                    extends
To the inside!

---

* The parrot. The parrot is not just considered a figure for a mimicker or a talkative, in Yoruba culture; it is also a symbol for an unbiased or truth talker—hence its name Ayek'ootọ, translating as 'The-World-Hates-Truth.'

[ARẸMU]

I may not know...

Life people stuff with many concepts
with many definitions
with many explanations
Love people give many different contexts
with many dimensions
but with many questions
But even when my mind doesn't get
their love classifying and complexity, my dear
I still know one thing for certain!
I still know one thing for certain!

Oh I may not know which is which
I may not know what's what
I may not know the who's who—
But I am sure I know you!

I may not know how
I may not know why
I may not know what
But I know I love you!
I know for sure I love you!

[ARẸWA]

True love among lovebirds

Like the bending of rainbow to kiss pretty earth—
Or the blending of deep blue seas up into light
                                                blue skies
Or just like the lovely sun kiss on blossoming
                                                morning glory
so is true love
among lovebirds
so is one love
among twosomes

Like the sweet coos of pigeons to listening ear
And like stream ripples to happy-flapping
                                                duck and drake
Or like the warmth of cuddle love to two
                                                turtle doves—
so is one love
among two birds
and so is true love
among lovebirds

and much so
you are to me, love
and much so
I am to you!

[ARẸMU]

Love song

Is it sickness
That for nights I can't sleep?
Is it nervousness
That for days I can't speak?
There is this beautiful girl I love
But how to speak to her I don't know
There is this beautiful girl within my heart
But I've got butterflies in my stomach!

this song I will sing for you
this song I will sing for you
the song I have learnt from my mama
this song I will sing *for you!*

Is it sickness
That for nights I can't sleep?
Is it nervousness
That for days I can't speak?
There is this beautiful girl I love
But how to speak to her I don't know
There is this beautiful girl beneath my chest
But I've got butterflies in my stomach!

Can I find a good expression
for your lovely good looks Arẹwa**?
Are there ever apt words of description
for your endearing good character Awẹlẹwa**?
What farmer gets a God-sent rain and doesn't sing?
What man finds a virtuous woman and doesn't
                                                    rejoice?
And I am favoured by God to have found you!
I am favoured by God to have found you!

Ah take me to know your mama
she whose breast milk gave you nurture,
my love, my sister!
Take me to know your people
they in whose eyes you matured
they in whose hands you become woman!
Take us please to your village
Take us please to your people
our love, our sister!

Seven rivers, seven bridges
Seven borders, seven villages

---

* Beautiful lady.
** Lovely lady.

Ah, there is this beautiful girl I love
But how to say it to her people I don't know
There is this beautiful girl within my heart
But I've got butterflies in my stomach!

A bag of beads, a pot of kola nut
A gourd of palm wine, a keg of palm oil

Will I compare her price to pricey artifacts
only too soon bargained on the counter?
but *She* is more costly!
Will I compare her worth to precious cowries
only too soon exchanged in the export?
but *She* is more valued!
And a peerless jewel, a priceless gift
I have found in your daughter!

A peerless jewel, a priceless gift
He has found in our daughter
A peerless jewel, a priceless gift
He has found in our daughter

A peerless jewel, a priceless gift
I have found in you, my love, my sister!
A peerless jewel, a priceless gift
I have found in you, my love, my sister!

[ARẸMU]

Man talk

Like thunder your face is, Mister Ex
Guys won't talk behind their backs!
Uh, you're preparing to face-off with me?
Come let's meet
Face to face!

Like embers your eyeballs are
Man, guys look themselves in the eye!
An eye for an eye, did you say?
Come, let's see
Eyeball to eyeball!

But you've not been one to talk
things without a hearing
And men don't judge from a one-sided view!
It's one girl too many; and you want to come back?
Come, let's hear it
One-to-one!

Like thunder your face is, Mister Ex
Like embers your eyeballs are
But you've not been one to talk
things without a hearing
So, let's hear it
One-to-one!

Guys won't talk behind their backs!
Man, guys look themselves in the eye!
And men don't judge from a one-sided view!
So, let's see
Eyeball to eyeball!

Uh, you're preparing to face-off with me?
An eye for an eye, did you say?
It's one girl too many; and you want to come back?
Come and meet me
Face to face!

[ARẸWA]

It is you

You are the gift
Of God to me, I know for sure!
You are the best thing
That's ever happened to me, baby!
If I am to choose, if I am to choose a part
It is you I want to spend my life with, love!
It is you I want to spend my life with!

Old flames are gone out
The embers are doused
But the ashes remain
Past loves are gone with that 'past'
Past hates along with them
And a new love now burns
If I am to choose, if I am to choose a part
It is you I want to share my life with!
It is you I want to share my life with!

I wish you were my brother
Who came out from the groins
Of my father!
I wish you were my brother
Who came out from between the hips
Of my mother!
Oh you are my friend, you are my flame!
And it is you I want to be with the rest of my life!
It is you, baby!
It is you, I'm sure!

[ARẸMU]

Knight song

Now hear how sweetly the songbird
sings a sweet serenade.
Now look how beautifully the starry sky
twinkles a bedtime lamp.
Now feel the embrace of the cool breeze
rising from the streams over there to greet you.
And hear all Nature tonight joining me to whisper
Good night, my love...
        Sweet dreams.

The day-guard sun has gone off-duty
but the moon and the battalion stars
resume watch over lovely sleepy Earth.
The daylight songbirds have gone
to repose in their nests
but the night-bird now sings to you her lullaby...

        hear how sweetly the songbird
        sings a sweet serenade
        look how beautifully the starry sky
        twinkles a bedtime lamp
        hear how sweetly the songbird
        sings a sweet serenade

Oh, now I your knight too
will not be there for your nights too
and sing you a sweet serenade
but the ever-watching Eye keeps
the night watch for you.
So sleep well, my love…
          Sweet dreams.

For, I your knight should tomorrow
cross the ocean as you already know
in quest of pastures new overseas
and for the good of our lives together.
And you can rest very assured, my baby
that my heart will not repose there, my love
till I come back for you, my love…
          Good night.

[ARẸWA]

There are no words

Sorrow is not at its depths
When it can just be expressed
      With tears
Joy is not at its height
When it can only be expressed
      With laughter
Love is not at its best
When it can still be expressed
      In words…
      and there are no words to express
      how much I will miss you!
      and there are no words to say
      how much I love you!

[ARẸWA]

Till we meet again

We meet to part
We part, some day to meet perhaps
Till we meet again, my friend…
oh!

We meet many people we never feel their impact
We part with some people we'll for long feel
                                        their void
Friend, till we meet again…
oh no!

I wish I can follow you everywhere you're going
                                        now
Or that we can just continue to look at ourselves
But really, till we meet again…
mm!

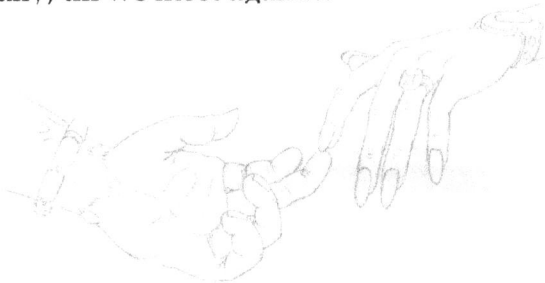

I want to hold back, but I would like to let go
I like to always gaze, but potted plants must
                              grow into trees outdoors
So... till we meet again Friend...
oh listen...

Positive influence is greater than promising
                                      affluence
And you're leaving me far better made today
                              than you first met me
And, oh, till we meet again my friend...

Mm, I'll really miss you!

iii. Retrospection

I don't really know
why I'm missing you so
vanished are words to explain
why the world is not the same again.

Since you left here
my mind longs after there
now in the dark I grope
keenly striving to cope.

Gbemisola Adeoti, *Naked Soles*, "Absence"*

---

* Used with permission of the author and copyright owner.

[ARĘWA]

Softly

Softly in the cool of evening
And from amid rows of trees like standing sentries
Waving to the winds whistling by
Birds sang their sweet, sweet notes
Softly in the calm of nightfall
From the splendid sky of colourful sunset
And with the gentle glow of mild sunshine
The gloaming lit the gathering gloom
Softly in the still of dusk
And as the sun released its warm clasp
From around sleepy Earth
The cool streams just hummed their lullaby
…And softly in the quiet of twilight
My love, handing out to me one
lovely love rose, and a love ring
In his badly bruised, spike-pierced, heroic hand...
He whispered to me
      I love you.

[THE AYEK'OOTQ BIRD]

Two turtle doves

By a stream side, two turtle doves
Were taking a sweet stroll of love.
The young duo smiled at each other,
For there was no cause for bother.
Then at once, the sweet female bird
Changed in her look and tone, and said:
Sweetie, yes I know you love me —
But will you still, when fades beauty?

Even if a plucking-off becomes of all these plumes,
He said, I will love you… so long as it is still YOU!

[AREWA]

I promise

Every night falls
With me forlornly peering into the street
Looking out for your return steps
Every day dawns
With me dreaming about you and pining away
But remembering your return promise
Every week passes
Not without the tempter's attempting voice
Cooing through my window at night
Oh you're staying too long behind, king of
                                    my castle!

Remember
You promised!

But then, after that old flame's fire is out
After my rising waves calm
After your long, long being away ends, my love
You'll still see me truly waiting
I promise!

iv. Inflection

'If I hold her hand
          She says, "Don't touch!"
If I hold her foot
          She says, "Don't touch!"
But when I hold her waist beads
          She pretends not to know.'

Chinua Achebe, *Things Fall Apart*

[ARẸWA]

Raw

yesterday yes yesterday wed-
nes…day yes wednesday twilight wednesday
…really looks like looks
like i'm beginning to fall for
him after all!

oh yes yesterday
twilight yesterday wednesday
'can still see him wind quietly, daringly
to my window yesterday
wednesday and coo again
through my windowpane
But
…no no!

yes his oh my! his broad broad
shoulders deep rough deep
voice oh my goodness! his hard
hard iron pinning someone down his
keen masculine keen penetrating
perfume poured inside me as i
just opened my secret door for
him after all…
God! what are you thinking girl!

come on be sensible you're
engaged girl! i'm marrying soon what's wrong?
but soon yes no date no date just as
soon as my prince charming returns for
his sweetheart here from his quest for pastures new
in faraway kings-town or king-dome
and then returns with me... to live
our happily-ever-after there! but
But
...no.

what the hell! who knows what
he is up to there too? yes
how am i so sure so sure he's not seeing
somebody else too how am i so
sure? so sure!
But
...ok-ay!

...Ugh
you're staying too long behind
king of my castle
these tempting advances here are
are killing me! you're staying too long behind
king of my castle but remember your
promise uh?
these tempting advances
are killing me! but you know i
promised i'll wait for you
these tempting advances are
are killing me! but you know i—
...Ugh!

what the hell! what the freaking hell!
wake up girl! it's 21st century! freaking 21st century!
love is game people say!
and i can well play along!
free world!

... oh yes yesterday twilight
oh twilight yesterday
'can still see him wind quietly, daringly
to my window yesterday
oh his goodness me! his deep rough
deep voice broad broad shoulders
eh my goodness! his hard hard iron
pinning someone down his
keen masculine keen penetrating
perfume poured inside me as i
just opened my secret door for
him after all…
God! what are you thinking girl!

look me! refined genteel refined
lady and raw thoughts raw thoughts raw
girlish instincts only repressed
for long in femininity canister!
God nah una fire wey dey refine i need o
mey e comot dis dirti' inside out a' beg!
no more dis…dis 'refined rawness'! But
but…

oh his my goodness! his hard hard
iron pinning someone down his
keen masculine keen penetrating
perfume poured inside me as i
just opened my secret door for
him after all…

and yes he said yes he said…so
sweet he said he said
i love You …

Oh…boy! I think I'm in love!

v. Reflection

The expense of spirit in a waste of shame
Is lust in action...
Before, a joy proposed; behind, a dream.
Shakespeare, Sonnet 129

[THE AYEK'OOTO BIRD]

The beauteous Rose flower

Look at the sad tale of this beauteous Rose,
how handsome Lust, charmed by her sweet beauty,

just with impulsive desire
plucked her onto his breast, cooing:

I love you.

And then he rashly unbuttoned the Rose's petal
                                                    clothes,
cast off her folds, tasted of her secret nectar at once.

And what is more? His appetite filled, his fancy
ended, our friend passed on from there, notoriously
                                                    hissing…

I had you.

[THE AYEK'OOTỌ BIRD]

Lovelust

She fell for *him* with her heart
He loved her with his mind
She fell for the old flame
While her real love
Went out for a while.

Do not argue; do not debate her
If she tells you what *he* tells her
That love is never real; never was.
Do not argue when they can't find.
One knew lust, the other love lost.

[THE AYEK'OOTỌ BIRD]

Life of ironies

The beggar sleeps in the cold night, unsheltered:
The rich man suffers from insomnia in bed.

The barren woman adopts another woman's kid:
School girls flush their fetuses into polythene bags.

The adolescent virgin is tired of keeping herself:
The womanizing guy is wishing to marry a virgin
when he's through.

Life!

Some people work, some people eat;
Some people steal from what is reaped.

Some babies die, some kiddies die;
Some people live as if they will never leave!

Some people keep chaste, some people keep lose;
Some people wonder if there's a tomorrow to
protect!

Some people rape, some people eagerly open laps —
And they forget there's always an 'after' waiting…
Or piling!

[ARẸWA]

Like after-rain radiance

As thunders rumble in my sombre soul
Like deep sighs sounding in the heavy clouds —
This gloomy thunderstorm
Let it calm!
Ah, let it calm!

Like teardrops falling from the sky
And raindrops falling from my eyes —
Ah, this stormy rain
Let it cease!
God, let it cease!

Like after-rain radiance beaming from the sky
Like after-pain sunshine gleaming from the eyes —
A cloudless gleam
Let it glow!
Please God, let it glow still!!

vi. Perfection

Angela's heart swelled. At last, she had an answer. A beautiful calm filled her. She blinked her tears away, handed her bouquet to Leigh, and turned back to her beloved. Their gaze met. She smiled. Hosea's hand tightened on hers, and together they walked up the steps to the allur.

Dorothy Clark, *Hosea's Bride**

---

* Used with permission of Steeple Hill Books, New York.

[ARẸWA]

As I am

There is no point in you
Seeing with love's illusory sight
A sacred goddess
Where only a human is, love!
There is no point, now
Seeing with love's veiled eyes
A sparkling angel
Where only a woman is!
There is no point at this point
Proving myself to be that perfect fantasy
That I never was!
For once, at least, for once, baby
Please open your eyes…
And see me
just as I am!

Now look at me with clear eyes
And let love's eyes now see, yet pardon!
Look at me; listen to me please
See, I'm naked of all pretensions!
Look at me, please — and if it startles you to see me
Far less perhaps than as I've existed in your

mind's eye

Oh please, please close your eyes…
And take me
just as I am …

[ARẸMU]

I do

If you scarce find it in your heart
to forgive yourself
      I have.
If no man has ever so much
accepted you just the way you are
      I will.
If you barely could see any longer
why anyone should see an angel in you
      I do.
And if I never since have told you
that I love you regardless
      … I do.

If no one knows how it feels to be forlorn
the way you've been before my return
      I know.
If no one knew the feeling of fighting hard
                      temptations
the way you once battled those tempting seductions
      I knew.
If I haven't since told you
that you are still my angel, my love
      I do.
And if I never since have told you
that I will love you ever more
      … I do!

* * *

Do you take this woman today
To be your wife
To love her
And cherish her
For better or for worse
For richer or for poorer
In sickness and in health
And all the days of your lives
Till death do you part?

… I Do!

[THE CHOIR]

Love

Beautiful, heavenly;
Wonderful, lovély;
So sweet serenély
      You can't it shove:
Controlling, possessing;
Delightfully pressing;
And feelings expressing,
      Is love, true love.

Marvellous, so wondrous;
Superb, splendiferous;
So great and mysterious
      Nothing can prove:
Gripping you, filling you;
Running all your veins through;
And charging the heart too,
      Is love, true love.

Angelic, seraphic;
Noble and romantic;
Sacred, divine, unique —
      Gi'en from above:
E'er unconditional;
Ne'er dying, eternal...
Love's inexplicable!
      And God is love!

vii. Repression

A few years pass after settling down in marriage with a kid. And due to some vicissitudes of marital life arising along the way, sadly separation is resorted to. Heartfelt yearnings are put into notes here but unfortunately remain, and still remain, unsent! Out of some fear that the other party may actually be cold, hard, or adamant, they said! But what if their fears were faced, their egos pocketed, and the letters were sent (or maybe sent Tomorrow)? Perhaps, this love story they make may have continued... indeed renascent and resurgent... from where it ends.

[Author's Note]

My beloved put his hand
By the latch of the door,
And my heart yearned for him.
I arose to open for my beloved,
And my hands dripped with myrrh,
My fingers with liquid myrrh,
On the handles of the lock.

I opened for my beloved,
But my beloved had turned away and was gone.
My heart leaped up when he spoke....
I charge you, O daughters of Jerusalem,
If you find my beloved,
That you tell him I am lovesick!

Solomon the King, Song of Songs*

---

* V.4 – 6 & 8, NKJV.

[ARẸWA]

You and me

At a distance
Several different colours of light
Sweetly combine to form a rainbow band
At a distance
Colourful rainbow in the sky,
Bending, embraces the stark earth beneath
At a distance
The light blue sky above
Kisses the deep blue sea below
But here, man will keep man
At a distance!

Two predators may well coexist
And even man and beast well can—
How much more
man and man?
Two ends of one spiral spring can at times meet
And even opposite poles of magnet do attract—
How much more
guy and girl?
Two lovebirds** may prove the
best of friends at parting
And even a pair of turtle doves
is, in everyday living—
How much more
you and me!?

---

* In this sense, a species of African parrot said to pine away when it loses its mate.

Why, if all Nature sings harmony
Then let our human nature, too, say anything but
                                                    discord;
For if opposites do coexist peacefully in nature
Then why should man and man fight in the world?
So then, like rainbow colours
Harmonize into a band
In such a pleasant combination
And the blues of the sky and the sea
Blend together in the distance
In such merging into each other
So also let's blend differences together
Harmonize discrepancies sweetly
Merge distinctions into one...
In close friendship, my dear
between
You and me!

[Note Unsent]

[ỌMỌLẸWA]

Love letter of a broken-hearted kid

Every morning
you woke me with a kiss
every evening
we went walking in the fields
every night
i played and played in your lap
till i slept off and still dreamt about you
but i never dreamt never dreamt
i would wake up one day
and won't see you nomore!

oh daddy come back!
couldn't guess why you and mummy had to part!
your baby girl's crying!
oh daddy why not come back today!?

every morning
i miss your lovely kiss
every evening
i look out to the streets for your coming
every night
i wake up to hear mummy
cry and cry so badly for you
but i never knew never knew
i will wake up today
and not see you still!

oh daddy come back please!
wouldn't know what mummy did to hurt you
but your baby loves you daddy!
please come together today...
at least because of me!

[Note Unsent]

[ARẸMU]

To his wool-white Dove

Do not consider my colour, my Dove,
  how that I am black — on this only look:
  that I lie longing by this little brook,
wanting your companionship on my cove!
Regard not this guise! But take me, your love
  though lacking your plumage! Ah, do not look
  on me from afar, for silence Cain took
for disdain! But I want you, for above
all your whiteness I have loved! So now, come —
  come near, O my love; keep me company!
    Come before this sun goes to sleep and day
for night paves way, and darkness overcomes
  this earth; and before these glows grow weary,
    and our hearth cold — O, come back; do not
                                          delay!

[Note Unsent]

[ARẸWA]

Forlornly

Seems confidant becomes cold
Who has been warm and friendly
Seems Friend chooses to be detached
Who has once cared with interest
We now turn mere acquaintances
Who have once been intimate friends
And maybe this fault isn't altogether
                                his for real! Ugh…!
But You won't do love-you-and-leave-you,
                                too, my Jesus
will You?

Obafemi Awolowo University Campus
November 2012

Acknowledgements

I hope those who have helped in bringing this book to completion from writing through production would allow me to say thank you publicly. I really want to thank my lovely sweetheart and a fellow poet too, Omotola. Thanks for your love, encouragement and valuable suggestions all along. I'm hoping to see your sensational work in print too, soon, dear. I want to say a big thank you to Prof Gbemisola Adeoti for reviewing the manuscript with rapt interest, and taking the time to write a wonderful forward note. I appreciate this sir; thank you. I also want to really thank my brother-in-law and my big sister Akin and Bukola Akinyemi, for taking an especial interest in this particular work and promoting it with Syncterface Media publishing house. Thank you for seeing in it something even far more than I saw. Thank you all.